THIS BOOK
BELONGS TO

....

....

I can't tell you how grateful I am that you decided to read my book. My most heartfelt thanks that you took time out of your life to choose my work and I hope you find benefit within these pages.

There are so many books available today that offer similar content so that makes it even more humbling that you decided to buying mine.

Tell me what you thought! I am eager to hear your opinion and ideas on what you read as are others who are looking for a good book to buy. Leave a review on Amazon.com so others can benefit from your wisdom!

With much thanks.

©COPYRIGHT 2024

The content contained within this book may not be reproduced, duplicated, or transmitted without direct written permission from the author or the publisher. Under no circumstances will any blame or legal responsibility be held against the publisher, or author, for any damages, reparation, or monetary loss due to the information contained within this book. Either directly or indirectly.

Legal Notice:
This book is copyright protected. This book is only for personal use. You cannot amend, distribute, sell, use, quote, or paraphrase any part, or the content within this book, without the consent of the author or publisher.

Disclaimer Notice:
Please note the information contained within this document is for educational and entertainment purposes only. All effort has been executed to present accurate, up-to-date, and reliable, complete information. No warranties of any kind are declared or implied. Readers acknowledge that the author is not engaging in the rendering of legal, financial, medical, or professional advice. The content within this book has been derived from various sources. Please consult a licensed professional before attempting any techniques outlined in this book. By reading this document, the reader agrees that under no circumstances is the author responsible for any losses, direct or indirect, which are incurred as a result of the use of the information contained within this document, including, but not limited to — errors, omissions, or inaccuracies.

Table of Contents

What is a Money Broker?	6
Chapter 1: Understanding the Money Broker Industry	8
Chapter 2: Developing the Skills and Knowledge Required	12
Chapter 3: Setting Up Your Money Broker Business	18
Chapter 4: Building a Network of Lenders and Clients	25
Chapter 5: The Loan Application Process	30
Chapter 7: Managing and Growing Your Money Broker Business	39
Chapter 8: Overcoming Challenges and Building Long-Term Success	45
Chapter 9: Setting Up the Loan Application	53
Chapter 10: How Do Money Brokers Get Paid?	68
Final Words	77

Introduction

Are you looking to make a six-figure income and start your own business? Becoming a money broker may be the perfect opportunity for you. This book will guide aspiring money brokers on how to earn $100,000 per year by assisting clients in finding low-interest rate loans. It covers understanding the industry, developing necessary skills, setting up a business, building a network of lenders and clients, navigating the loan application process, negotiating for low-interest rates, managing and growing the business, overcoming challenges, and building long-term success. With practical tips and strategies as well as resources included throughout this book; it emphasizes that there is potential for lucrative career opportunities in becoming a money broker.

This book begins by introducing the role of a money broker and providing an overview of the lucrative opportunities in this industry. We then discuss developing the skills and knowledge required to become a successful money broker such as financial literacy, communication, negotiation, market trends, and loan rates. Moving on from that we provide information on how to set up your money broker business such as legal considerations, licensing requirements, branding, and more. Additionally, we provide strategies on how to build a network of lenders and clients through researching reputable lenders and financial institutions, approaching them, marketing your business, attracting clients and negotiating for low-interest rate loans.

Once you have established the basics for your business, this book will guide you on how to manage and grow your money broker business. We provide strategies for client relationship management, providing ongoing support and guidance to clients, expanding your network of lenders and clients, scaling your business, overcoming competition and staying ahead in the industry as well as adapting to changing market conditions and regulations. Finally, we discuss building a reputation for trust and reliability for long-term success.

At the end of this book, we provide resources such as sample loan application forms and documents, further learning opportunities and a glossary of key terms used in the money broker industry. We emphasize that this book is intended to provide guidance only; readers should consult with professionals and adhere to local regulations and laws when starting and operating a money broker business.

What is a Money Broker?

A money broker is a professional who acts as a middleman between borrowers and lenders. Essentially, they assist clients in finding low-interest rate loans that fit their needs and financial situation. This can involve a range of financial products, from mortgages to personal loans and beyond.

The role of a money broker is not only important but also lucrative. With the ever-increasing demand for loans, the industry presents a lot of opportunities for those who have the skills to match borrowers with lenders. Some of the most successful brokers earn upwards of $100,000 per year.

By working with clients to understand their needs, financial situation, and credit score, brokers can match them with the best possible loan options. They then negotiate favorable terms and rates with lenders on behalf of their clients. In exchange for their services, brokers receive a commission from the lender.

One of the key benefits of working with a money broker is their ability to find low-interest rate loans that might otherwise be difficult to secure. This can save clients a lot of money over the long term, making it a valuable service for anyone looking to borrow money.

The role of a money broker is to help clients find the best possible loan options for their needs and financial situation. With the potential to earn a significant income and provide a valuable service to clients, it's no wonder that more and more people are entering this growing industry.

By reading this book, readers will gain a comprehensive understanding of the money broker industry and the potential to become a successful money broker. Readers will be given practical tips, strategies, and resources to set up their own businesses and develop the necessary skills required for success. This includes information on legal considerations, licensing requirements, branding, managing and growing the business, developing a network of lenders and clients, navigating the loan application process, negotiating for low-interest rates, overcoming competition, staying ahead in the industry, and building a reputation for trust and reliability.

We encourage readers to take action and pursue their journey in the money broker industry. With dedication and hard work comes success; we wish you the best of luck in becoming a profitable money broker.

Let's get started!

Chapter 1: Understanding the Money Broker Industry

The financial services industry is a dynamic and multifaceted field that comprises various professionals who offer financial products, services, and advice to individuals, businesses, and institutions. One such profession is that of a money broker. This chapter will provide an in-depth understanding of the money broker industry, different types of brokers, and the benefits and advantages of becoming a money broker.

Overview of the Financial Services Industry

The financial services industry is a vast and complex world that includes numerous entities, such as banks, insurance companies, investment firms, credit unions, and brokerage firms. These entities work collaboratively to provide financial products and services to consumers. The primary goal of the financial services industry is to help individuals and businesses manage their money effectively and efficiently.

The industry encompasses a broad range of services, including banking, lending, insurance, investment, and financial planning. Moreover, it is heavily regulated by government bodies to ensure that financial institutions maintain proper standards and protect consumers' interests.

Different Types of Brokers

Money brokers are professionals who act as intermediaries between borrowers and lenders. They help clients find low-interest rate loans that fit their needs and financial situation. There are various types of brokers depending on the type of loan they specialize in. Some of the common types include:

Mortgage Brokers

Mortgage brokers specialize in helping clients secure mortgages for purchasing homes. They work with a variety of lenders and help their clients shop around for the best terms and rates. Mortgage brokers act as a link between mortgage lenders and borrowers, helping borrowers find the right mortgage product for their needs and financial situation.

Business Loan Brokers

Business loan brokers assist business owners in securing financing for their ventures. They help clients find loans that are tailored to their specific business needs. Business loan brokers have a broad network of lenders and can match business owners with the right financing solutions for their company.

Personal Loan Brokers

Personal loan brokers help individuals secure financing for personal needs such as debt consolidation, home improvements, or other expenses. They have access to a range of lenders and can help clients find the best terms and rates for their personal loan needs.

Benefits and Advantages of Becoming a Money Broker

Becoming a money broker is an attractive career option for individuals interested in finance. Some of the benefits and advantages of becoming a money broker include:

High Earning Potential

One of the primary advantages of becoming a money broker is the potential income. With the ever-increasing demand for loans, the industry presents a lot of opportunities for those who have the skills to match borrowers with lenders. Some of the most successful brokers earn upwards of $100,000 per year.

Flexibility

Another advantage of becoming a money broker is the flexibility of the job. Brokers can work independently or as part of a team. They can work from home or an office and set their own hours.

Helping Clients Achieve Their Goals

Becoming a money broker can be a rewarding career as it involves helping clients achieve their financial goals. By working with clients to understand their needs, financial situation, and credit score, brokers are able to match them with the best possible loan options. They then negotiate favorable terms and rates with lenders on behalf of their clients. In exchange for their services, brokers receive a commission from the lender.

The Demand for Low-Interest Rate Loans

One of the driving factors behind the demand for money brokers is the need for low-interest-rate loans. Clients are looking for ways to save money on interest payments over the long term. By working with a money broker, they can find loans with favorable rates and terms that might otherwise be difficult to secure.

Moreover, the demand for low-interest-rate loans is increasing due to the current economic climate. Many individuals and businesses are struggling financially due to the pandemic, and low-interest rate loans can help them manage their expenses.

The money broker industry is an exciting and lucrative field that offers a range of opportunities for those who have a passion for finance and helping clients secure the best possible loans. Whether you are interested in mortgages, business loans, or personal loans, there is a niche for you in this growing industry. Becoming a money broker can provide a high earning potential, flexibility, and the satisfaction of helping clients achieve their financial goals.

To get started in the money broker industry, it is essential to gain a comprehensive understanding of the industry and its various aspects. This involves familiarizing yourself with different types of brokers, the financial services market, government regulations, and other relevant information. Additionally, you must have an entrepreneurial mindset and be willing to work hard to succeed.

Money brokers can make a lot of money working from home. They look for the best loan deals for people and businesses and help them save money on interest payments. They work hard to match borrowers with lenders that offer good rates and terms. If they do a good job, they can earn more than $100,000 each year!

It can be challenging to get into the money broker industry, but it is possible. With the right knowledge, skills, and attitude, you can become a successful money broker. The key is to be proactive with your research, build your network of lenders and clients, understand government regulations, and stay motivated throughout the process.

Chapter 2: Developing the Skills and Knowledge Required

Becoming a successful money broker requires more than just passion and dedication. It involves developing the skills and knowledge necessary to successfully navigate the industry. In this chapter, we will discuss how to acquire these key skills and gain an understanding of the different aspects of the financial services market, government regulations, and other relevant information. We will also provide practical tips on setting up your business, building a network of lenders and clients, navigating the loan application process, negotiating for low-interest rates, managing and growing your business, overcoming challenges, and building long-term success in this lucrative field.

Identifying the necessary skills and traits for a successful money broker

Becoming a money broker requires a variety of important skills and traits. To be successful, money brokers must have an in-depth understanding of the various aspects of the industry such as financial services, banking regulations, loan processing procedures, credit scores, and more. Additionally, they must be able to network with a range of lenders, such as banks, credit unions, and other financial institutions.

Money brokers must also have excellent interpersonal skills so they can effectively communicate with clients and lenders. They should be able to explain complex information in simple terms to help borrowers understand their options when selecting the right loan for their needs. In addition, money brokers must have strong negotiation skills to secure the best terms and rates for their clients.

Lastly, money brokers should be self-motivated and have an entrepreneurial mindset. As it is a competitive industry, they must be able to think creatively and come up with innovative solutions when needed. They also need to stay focused on their goals even in the face of challenges and setbacks.

By leveraging the skills and traits listed above, money brokers can establish themselves as reliable source for low-interest rate loans that help clients save money over the long term. This can lead to lucrative opportunities in the industry and create lasting success.

Overview of financial literacy and knowledge of loan products

Money brokers are a valuable asset in the financial market. They specialize in connecting clients with lenders that offer low-interest rate loans, enabling them to save money over the long term. While this type of work has the potential to be lucrative, becoming a successful money broker requires more than just passion and dedication. It involves having an in-depth understanding of the financial market, loan types and products, credit scores, and other aspects of the industry.

The most important step in becoming a successful money broker is gaining a comprehensive understanding of the industry. This involves familiarizing yourself with different types of loans, such as mortgages, business loans, personal loans, and more. Additionally, it is important to have a strong understanding of credit scores and how they affect loan interest rates. Knowing the different government regulations that apply to money brokers is also essential, as these can have a major impact on any potential deals you make.

Finally, it is important to stay up-to-date with changes in the industry so you are aware of new products, regulations, and more. Investing in financial literacy is key for any money broker to have a successful career.

By developing a strong understanding of the industry and gaining necessary skills, you can set yourself up for success as a profitable money broker. With the right knowledge, dedication, and attitude, there are endless opportunities available in this lucrative field.

By leveraging the skills and traits listed above, money brokers can establish themselves as reliable source for low-interest rate loans that help clients save money over the long term. This can lead to lucrative opportunities in the industry and create lasting success. With practical tips, strategies, and resources available throughout this book, you can become a successful money broker and earn $100,000/year or more. Start your journey today to unlock the potential of this lucrative career!

Building strong communication and negotiation skills

Money brokers need to have strong interpersonal and negotiation skills to be successful. They must be able to effectively communicate with both clients and lenders, clearly explaining complex information in simple terms so that borrowers can understand their options when selecting a loan. Money brokers should also be comfortable negotiating for the best terms and rates on behalf of their clients to secure the best deal possible.

To hone these skills, money brokers should focus on developing their communication and negotiation techniques. This can be done through working with a mentor or taking courses in communication and negotiation. Additionally, they should practice active listening so that they understand what lenders and clients are looking for and make sure they are addressing all needs and concerns. By honing these skills, money brokers can become a reliable source of low-interest rate loans for their clients.

Setting up a business and building a network

An important part of becoming a successful money broker is setting up your own business and building a network of lenders and clients. This involves registering your business with the relevant authorities, ensuring you meet all legal requirements. Additionally, it is important to create a professional website and other channels such as social media to market your services and attract potential clients.

Money brokers must also actively build their own network of lenders so they can access the best deals for their clients. This involves reaching out and networking with banks, credit unions, and other financial institutions. Money brokers should also focus on building relationships with their clients so they can better understand their needs and find the best loan for them.

By setting up a business and building a strong network of lenders and clients, money brokers set themselves up for long-term success as a reliable source of low-interest rate loans.

Navigating the loan application process and managing/growing your business

Once you have established yourself as a money broker, it is important to understand how the loan application process works to secure the best deals for your clients. This involves understanding different loan types, credit scores and their impact on interest rates, legal requirements, and more.

Once the loan is approved, money brokers must be able to manage their business effectively to ensure customer satisfaction. This includes staying on top of paperwork, managing client expectations, keeping up-to-date with regulations and changes in the industry, and more. Money brokers should also focus on growing their business by looking for new clients and expanding their network of lenders.

By navigating the loan application process and managing/growing your business, money brokers can develop a successful career as a reliable source of low-interest rate loans that help clients save money over the long term.

Learning about market trends and loan rates

Money brokers must also stay informed about market trends and loan rates. Keeping up-to-date with changes in the industry is essential for success as a money broker, as this allows them to provide their clients with the best terms and rates available. This includes tracking macroeconomic conditions, such as employment rates and inflation, as well as local economic trends. Money brokers should also monitor the loan rates offered by different banks and credit unions to find the best deal for their clients.

By staying informed about market trends and loan rates, money brokers can better serve their clients and maximize their earning potential.

Overcoming challenges

The role of a money broker is not without its challenges. Money brokers must be able to navigate a competitive industry and manage their business to remain profitable. They should also stay informed about changes in the market and regulations so they can effectively negotiate on behalf of their clients.

Money brokers must have strong problem-solving skills to overcome any obstacles that arise. This includes understanding how to effectively handle difficult clients, navigating complex legal requirements, and dealing with rejection. Additionally, money brokers should have a positive attitude and remain motivated to stay successful in the industry.

By developing strong problem-solving skills and maintaining a positive outlook, money brokers can successfully overcome any challenges that come their way.

Building long-term success as a money broker

Money brokers have the potential to build successful, long-term careers in the industry. This involves developing strong communication and negotiation skills, setting up their own business and building a network of lenders and clients, navigating the loan application process, managing/growing their business, staying informed about market trends and loan rates, and overcoming challenges.

By following the steps outlined in this book, aspiring money brokers can become profitable professionals in a lucrative industry. With dedication and hard work, they can look forward to building long-term success as a reliable source of low-interest rate loans for their clients.

Chapter 3: Setting Up Your Money Broker Business

Legal considerations and licensing requirements

Setting up a money broker business is an important step for aspiring money brokers to take to achieve success. It involves understanding the legal considerations and licensing requirements associated with it, as well as other essential elements such as registering the business, creating a professional website, managing finances, and obtaining insurance.

Legal Considerations

The first step in setting up a money broker business is to understand the legal considerations and licensing requirements. This includes understanding the regulations and laws that apply in each state, as well as any federal regulations. Money brokers must also make sure they have the necessary license to operate legally in their area.

Registering Your Business

Once you know what is required of you legally, the next step is to register your business. This involves choosing a business name and filing the necessary paperwork with the relevant authorities. It is important to research and understand the different types of business structures available to choose the one that best suits your needs.

Setting up a Professional Website

In addition to registering your business, setting up a professional website is essential to establishing a successful money broker business. A website allows potential clients and lenders to learn more about your services and network with you online. It should include information about the company, its mission statement, contact details, and other relevant information to attract customers and build trust.

Managing Finances

Money brokers must be able to effectively manage their finances to remain profitable and stay on top of their expenses. This involves understanding the financial regulations governing money brokers, keeping accurate records of transactions and payments, budgeting, and more. Money brokers should also familiarize themselves with various financial tools such as accounting software which can help them better manage their finances.

Obtaining Insurance

Money brokers should also obtain the necessary insurance to protect themselves and their business from any potential risks or liabilities. This includes errors and omissions insurance, which covers mistakes made while providing services, as well as general liability insurance, which covers accidents and damage caused by the money broker's services.

By understanding and following the necessary legal considerations, registering their businesses, setting up a professional website, managing finances, and obtaining insurance, money brokers can establish a successful business in the industry.

Choosing the right business structure (sole proprietorship, partnership, LLC)

Money brokers must choose the right business structure to remain compliant with applicable laws and regulations, as well as best suit their needs. The three main types of business structures are sole proprietorship, partnership, and limited liability company (LLC).

Sole Proprietorship

A sole proprietorship is a type of business owned and run by one individual. This type of business structure offers the advantage of simplicity and requires minimal paperwork to set up.

Partnership

A partnership is a business structure in which two or more individuals share ownership and management responsibilities. Partners are financially liable for any debts incurred by the business, so it is important to choose partners carefully.

Limited Liability Company (LLC)

An LLC is a type of business structure that provides limited liability for its owners. This means that the members' personal assets are protected from any debts or liabilities incurred by the company. It also offers flexible management options, making it an attractive choice for money brokers who want to manage their own businesses.

By understanding which business structure best suits their needs, money brokers can ensure that they remain compliant with applicable laws and regulations while maximizing the potential of their business.

Establishing a professional image and brand

With the potential for a lucrative career as a money broker, it is important for aspiring professionals to establish a professional image and brand. This involves understanding the market, developing industry-specific skills, networking with other professionals in the field, and building trust with clients.

Understanding the Market

It is essential for money brokers to understand the market to remain competitive, stay informed of trends and developments, and ensure that they are offering the best services possible. This includes understanding different types of loans and their respective advantages and disadvantages, researching lenders, studying industry news, and more.

Developing Industry-Specific Skills

Money brokers must develop a range of skills to be successful in the field. This includes being knowledgeable about different types of loans, understanding financial regulations, staying up-to-date on changing laws and regulations, managing finances effectively, and more.

Networking with Other Professionals

Money brokers should also make sure to network with other professionals in the industry. This includes attending industry conferences, joining professional organizations, and staying in touch with other money brokers.

Building Trust with Clients

Finally, it is important to build trust with clients. This involves being honest and transparent about services offered as well as fees charged. Money brokers should also be willing to answer any questions that clients may have and provide guidance throughout the loan application process.

By understanding the market, developing industry-specific skills, networking with other professionals, and building trust with clients, money brokers can establish a professional image and brand that will help them succeed in the field.

Creating an Effective Online Presence

In today's digital age, having an effective online presence is essential for any business. Money brokers should create an online presence that accurately reflects their services and brand to attract potential clients and build trust. This includes maintaining a professional website, creating social media accounts, developing content (such as blog posts, videos, etc.), engaging with customers online, and more.

Maintaining a Professional Website

Having a professional website is essential for money brokers. A website should include information about the company, its mission statement, contact details, and other relevant information to attract customers and build trust. The website should also be user-friendly and optimized for search engines to ensure maximum visibility.

Creating Social Media Accounts

Money brokers should also create social media accounts to connect with potential clients. This includes setting up accounts on platforms such as Facebook, Twitter, and Instagram. Social media can be used to post news, updates, offers, and other relevant information that will help engage customers and build relationships.

Developing Content

Developing content such as blog posts, videos, and other forms of media is also a great way to increase brand visibility and attract customers. Content should be relevant, informative, and engaging to ensure maximum engagement with potential clients.

Engaging with Customers Online

Finally, money brokers should engage with customers online. This includes responding to messages and comments promptly, following up on queries, providing guidance throughout the loan application process, and more.

By maintaining a professional website, creating social media accounts, developing content, and engaging with customers online, money brokers can create an effective online presence that will help them succeed in the field.

By understanding the legal requirements of setting up a business, establishing a professional image and brand, and creating an effective online presence, money brokers can ensure that they are set up for success. With the right knowledge and strategies in place, aspiring money brokers can build successful businesses with great potential for lucrative earnings.

Setting up a home office or leasing commercial space

Once a money broker has established their business, they must decide on either setting up a home office or leasing commercial space. Setting up a home office is often the most cost-effective solution for those just starting out and may provide more flexibility in terms of working hours.

When setting up a home office, money brokers should consider factors such as the type of equipment need, available space, internet access, and more. Money brokers should also ensure that they follow all applicable laws and regulations concerning home-based businesses.

Leasing commercial space may be beneficial for money brokers who are looking to expand their business or those who require a professional working environment with access to amenities such as meeting rooms and storage space. Money brokers should consider factors such as the size of the space, its location, accessibility, etc. when deciding on a commercial space.

By understanding their business needs and weighing the pros and cons of both options, money brokers can make an informed decision about whether to set up a home office or lease commercial space.

Successful money brokers must understand the industry, develop the necessary skills and knowledge, establish a professional image and brand, create an effective online presence, and make sure to follow laws and regulations concerning home-based businesses. With proper planning and dedication, aspiring money brokers can set up successful businesses with great potential for lucrative earnings.

Chapter 4: Building a Network of Lenders and Clients

Researching and identifying reputable lenders and financial institutions

Building a successful network of lenders and clients is essential for any money broker to succeed. To do so, it's important to research and identify reputable lenders and financial institutions. This can be done by utilizing online databases, researching industry publications, attending conferences, networking with other professionals, asking for recommendations from other brokers and banks, and more.

Money brokers should take into account factors such as the lender's terms and conditions, its loan products, fees charged, customer service, and more when researching lenders. This will help to ensure that all potential clients are offered competitive rates and services.

Developing relationships with lenders

Once a money broker has identified reputable lenders, they should develop relationships with them. This includes attending events and seminars hosted by lenders, engaging in conversations on social media, and more. Doing so will help money brokers to understand the lender's products and services better, connect with key decision-makers, and build a foundation of trust between the two parties.

Marketing and networking with potential clients

Money brokers should also market their services and network with potential clients. This can be done through various channels such as online advertisements, attending industry events, seminars, or workshops, creating a referral program, building relationships with other professionals in the same field (such as real estate agents), providing free consultations, and more. Doing so will help to build a strong client base and create more opportunities for business.

By researching potential lenders, developing relationships with them, and effectively marketing their services, money brokers can build a successful network of lenders and clients. Doing so will enable them to provide their clients with the best possible loan products and services which will in turn lead to increased profits for the broker.

Money brokers should research potential lenders, develop relationships with them, and network with potential clients to build a successful network of lenders and clients. Doing so will enable money brokers to provide their clients with the best possible loan products and services which will lead to increased profits for the broker. With proper planning and dedication, money brokers can ensure that they are set up for long-term success.

Approaching lenders and building relationships

Money brokers should take proactive steps to build relationships with lenders and network with potential clients. This involves engaging in conversations with lenders, attending industry events and conferences, maintaining a professional website, creating social media accounts, developing content, providing free consultations to potential clients, and more.

When approaching lenders, money brokers should be prepared to discuss their business services, qualifications, and experience in the industry. This will help to establish credibility and trust between the money broker and lender. Money brokers should also use online tools such as social media platforms to communicate with lenders, potential clients, and other stakeholders in the loan process.

Money brokers should be proactive in building relationships with lenders and networking with potential clients to ensure that their business grows and remains profitable over the long term. With proper planning and dedication, money brokers can build successful relationships with lenders and create a strong client base.

Strategies for attracting and acquiring clients

Money brokers should utilize several strategies to attract and acquire clients. This includes providing an online presence by creating a professional website; engaging in conversations with potential clients on social media platforms; sending out email campaigns, SMS messages, or direct mailers; hosting seminars or webinars; offering free consultations; leveraging word of mouth marketing from existing clients or other stakeholders in the loan process; and more.

Money brokers should identify their target market and tailor their strategies to meet the needs of these clients. Additionally, they should focus on providing valuable services such as timely communication, follow-up, high customer service standards, etc. These strategies will help to ensure that money brokers attract and retain profitable clients.

By utilizing the strategies discussed, money brokers can attract and acquire profitable clients and build a successful business. With proper planning and dedication, money brokers can ensure that their businesses remain profitable over the long term.

Utilizing marketing and advertising techniques

Money brokers must utilize a range of marketing and advertising techniques to ensure their business succeeds. These methods can include utilizing online platforms such as social media, website development and optimization, search engine optimization (SEO), email campaigns, direct mailers, content marketing, video promotions, etc. Money brokers should create relevant and engaging content that resonates with their target audience to capture the attention of potential clients.

Money brokers should also consider utilizing a range of traditional advertising techniques such as print media, radio and television commercials, telephone campaigns, etc. Doing so will help to maximize the reach of money broker services and increase their client base. Additionally, money brokers should take advantage of opportunities for free advertising by attending events, industry seminars, or workshops.

By utilizing a range of marketing and advertising techniques, money brokers can broaden their reach and increase their client base. With proper planning and dedication, money brokers can ensure that they are set up for long-term success.

Setting up the necessary infrastructure

Money brokers should also ensure that their business has the necessary infrastructure in place. This includes setting up an office or workspace; establishing a customer relationship management (CRM) system; purchasing necessary software, hardware, and equipment; creating a website; setting up accounting software to track financials; hiring staff; and more. Money brokers should research various options when selecting their infrastructure to ensure they are getting the best quality for their budget.

By setting up the necessary infrastructure, money brokers can provide a consistent and reliable service to their clients which will help to build trust and loyalty. Doing so will also enable money brokers to scale up their business as it grows over the long term.

Chapter 5: The Loan Application Process

Guiding clients through the loan application process

Money brokers must be well-versed in the loan application process to better assist their clients. The loan application process can vary depending on the type of loan, but generally involves several key steps.

First, money brokers should ensure that their clients have completed all necessary paperwork and gathered the required documents from lenders. The documents needed for the loan application process typically include income statements, tax returns, bank statements, credit reports, asset and liability statements, etc.

Once the paperwork is completed, money brokers should review the information with their clients to make sure all details are accurate. Money brokers should also provide advice and guidance throughout the loan application process to ensure that their clients are making the best financial decisions.

Once the loan application is submitted, money brokers should be proactive in communicating with lenders and following up on requests for additional documents or information. Money brokers should also provide updates to their clients regarding the status of their loan application. During this process, money brokers should aim to negotiate for lower interest rates and better terms for their client.

By guiding clients through the loan application process, money brokers can ensure a smooth and successful experience for both lender and borrower.

Preparing necessary documents and paperwork

Money brokers should become familiar with the legal and regulatory requirements of the loan application process to ensure that they are in compliance with all applicable laws. Money brokers should be proactive in understanding industry policies, filing documents with regulators, and providing the necessary disclosures to their clients.

In addition, money brokers should thoroughly review all loan terms and conditions, so they can provide sound advice to their clients. Money brokers should also ensure that all required paperwork is completed and filed accurately to move the process along smoothly.

By preparing necessary documents and paperwork, money brokers can help ensure a successful loan application process for both lender and borrower. Doing so will also help protect the interests of both parties and demonstrate the money broker's expertise.

Understanding credit scores and their impact on loan applications

Money brokers should also understand the importance of credit scores when it comes to loan applications. Credit scores are numerical representations of an individual's or business's creditworthiness. These scores are based on a variety of factors such as payment history, loan types, amounts owed, length of credit history, etc.

Money brokers should be familiar with the different credit scoring models used by lenders to provide tailored advice to their clients. This includes understanding what aspects of a credit score can help or hurt an individual's loan application and providing guidance on how to improve these scores over time.

By understanding credit scores and their impact on loan applications, money brokers can provide informed advice to their clients and increase the likelihood of a successful loan application.

Tips for improving clients' creditworthiness

Money brokers should provide their clients with the necessary tools and strategies to improve their creditworthiness. Money brokers can help their clients build a strong credit history by providing valuable information and advice on how to manage debt, establish a budget, pay bills on time, and more.

Money brokers should also explain the importance of having a good credit score and the consequences of not managing debt responsibly. Money brokers can also provide advice on how to dispute errors in credit reports, use credit cards strategically, and other tactics that can help improve clients' credit scores over time.

By helping their clients understand the importance of good credit and providing tips for improving creditworthiness, money brokers can increase the likelihood of successful loan applications and create a more sustainable business.

Becoming a profitable money broker is no easy feat, but with the right tips, strategies, and resources, it can be an incredibly rewarding career. Money brokers should understand the industry fundamentals, ensure that they have the necessary infrastructure in place, guide clients through the loan application process, and provide advice on improving creditworthiness. By doing so, money brokers can build a successful business that provides value to both lenders and borrowers alike.

Chapter 6: Negotiating Low-Interest Rate Loans

As a money broker, one of the most important skills to have is the ability to negotiate and secure low-interest rate loans for your clients. Negotiating low-interest rates can be a tricky process but with the right knowledge and strategies, it can be done successfully. In this chapter, we will explore how money brokers can effectively negotiate for low-interest rate loans by understanding key industry terms, leveraging relationships with lenders, utilizing available resources, and more. By learning these tactics and applying them in practice, money brokers can maximize their earning potential while providing value to their clients.

Techniques for negotiating with lenders on behalf of clients

Money brokers should approach negotiations with lenders on behalf of their clients in a professional and methodical manner. Money brokers should be prepared to explain the situation and provide evidence for why their client qualifies for a lower interest rate loan. Money brokers should also be prepared to address any questions or concerns that the lender may have.

Money brokers should leverage their relationships with lenders to negotiate lower interest rates for their clients. Money brokers can use their existing network of contacts to establish a rapport with lenders and demonstrate the value they bring as a reliable partner in the loan application process.

In addition, money brokers should research available resources that may provide insights into current market rates and trends. By understanding the current interest rate environment, money brokers can gain an advantage in negotiations with lenders on behalf of their clients. Money brokers should also use industry-specific terms and language to demonstrate a familiarity with the industry and establish credibility as an expert in the field.

Finally, money brokers should be prepared to make compromises to reach an agreement with lenders. Money brokers should be mindful of their clients' interests and ensure that any concessions made are done in a way that still serves the best interest of their client.

By using these negotiation techniques, money brokers can successfully secure low-interest rate loans for their clients while maximizing their earning potential as a money broker. Money brokers should also prepare themselves to handle any challenges or roadblocks that may arise in the process and remain confident and persistent throughout negotiations. With the right tools, strategies, and resources, money brokers can become successful and profitable in the industry.

Understanding loan terms, interest rates, and repayment options

Money brokers should be knowledgeable in the specific terms, conditions, and interest rates associated with loans to make informed decisions for their clients. Money brokers should understand the various types of loans available such as secured and unsecured loans, fixed-rate or variable-rate loans, and short-term or long-term loans.

Money brokers should also be aware of different repayment options such as fixed monthly payments, balloon payments, and interest-only payments. Money brokers should understand the implications of each repayment option on their clients' budgets and financial health.

Additionally, money brokers should be familiar with the factors that lenders consider when setting interest rates including credit scores, loan-to-value ratios, debt-to-income ratios, and collateral. Money brokers can use this knowledge to their advantage in negotiations with lenders on behalf of their clients.

By understanding the various terms, conditions and repayment options associated with loans, money brokers can provide valuable advice to their clients while making better decisions for their business. With the right knowledge and strategies, money brokers can improve their chances of securing low-interest rate loans for their clients and achieving long-term success in the industry.

Strategies for securing the best loan deals for clients

Money brokers can use a variety of strategies to secure the best loan deals for their clients. Money brokers should have an in-depth knowledge of their clients' financial situation, including creditworthiness and debt-to-income ratio, so that they can accurately assess their eligibility for various loan products and interest rates.

Money brokers should also take the time to compare loan products from multiple lenders to find the best deals for their clients. Money brokers should be familiar with different terms and repayment options so they can further negotiate for lower interest rates with lenders.

In addition, money brokers should leverage their network of contacts within the industry to secure discounts and other incentives on behalf of their clients. Money brokers can also use their existing relationships with lenders to quickly process loan applications and increase the chances of securing favorable terms. By using all these strategies, money brokers can provide valuable services to their clients while increasing their earning potential as a successful money broker.

Handling counteroffers and closing the deal

Money brokers should be prepared to handle counteroffers from lenders when negotiating for the best loan deals for their clients. Money brokers can evaluate counteroffers based on the terms and conditions, interest rates, repayment options, and other financial benefits that come with the loan. Money brokers should then use their expertise to compare and contrast the different offers and determine which one best meets their clients' needs.

Money brokers should also remain professional and courteous throughout negotiations as this will increase their chances of successfully closing a deal. Money brokers should take the time to listen to lenders' concerns and understand their perspective before responding with a counteroffer or making a final decision. This can help establish trust between money brokers and lenders, which may lead to more favorable terms in future negotiations.

Finally, money brokers should always remain focused on their goal of securing the best loan deals for their clients while remaining mindful of any risks involved with taking out a loan. Money brokers must weigh the short-term gain of obtaining favorable terms against any potential long-term consequences such as high interest payments or defaulting on payments. By using these strategies and exercising due diligence, money brokers can successfully negotiate for low-interest rate loans while mitigating any associated risks.

Becoming a successful and profitable money broker requires knowledge of the industry, understanding loan terms and repayment options, leveraging negotiation strategies with lenders, handling counteroffers professionally, and exercising due diligence when closing deals. By utilizing these techniques in combination with their expertise and network contacts within the industry, aspiring money brokers can maximize their earning potential while providing valuable services to clients. With dedication and hard work, you too can become a successful money broker who earns over $100k/year!

Chapter 7: Managing and Growing Your Money Broker Business

For aspiring money brokers, the goal is not only to make a living but also to build a profitable business. Becoming successful as a money broker requires more than just knowledge of the industry and negotiation skills—it also involves managing and growing your business. In this chapter, we will discuss how to effectively manage and grow your money broker business so that you can achieve long-term success in the industry. You'll learn about setting up systems for tracking clients, building relationships with lenders, expanding your services beyond loans, creating marketing strategies for attracting new customers, setting goals for growth and profitability, staying organized while juggling multiple projects at once, hiring help when needed, and other important tips from experienced professionals. With these strategies in hand you'll be well on your way towards becoming an established money broker who earns $100k/year or more!

Implementing effective client relationship management strategies

Money brokers must develop effective client relationship management strategies to build and maintain successful relationships with their clients. Money brokers should strive to understand their clients' goals, needs, and financial situation to provide tailored advice and better negotiate on their behalf. Money brokers should also be upfront about fees and other potential costs associated with the loan process, so that clients can make informed decisions. Money brokers should also keep track of client information such as loan applications, credit reports, loan contracts, and other documents related to the loan process to better serve their clients.

Client relationships are built over time through communication and trust. Money brokers should take the initiative to contact existing clients regularly to stay up-to-date on their financial situation and current needs. This will allow money brokers identify new opportunities for them such as refinancing or consolidating debt. Additionally, money brokers should actively cultivate new relationships by attending industry events or networking sessions where they can meet potential lenders or borrowers. By connecting with industry contacts through social media platforms such as LinkedIn or Twitter, money brokers can create a more extensive network which can result in more business opportunities for them.

Money brokers should always strive to provide value to their existing customers while continually seeking out new ones. By creating a positive experience for both lenders and borrowers while delivering results that exceed expectations, money brokers can build long-lasting relationships with key players within the industry while increasing profitability for their businesses.

Providing ongoing support and guidance to clients

Money brokers must provide ongoing support and guidance to their clients throughout the loan process. Money brokers should be available for consultation with their clients both before and after a loan has been secured. This will ensure that clients have all the information they need to make informed decisions on their financial matters.

Money brokers should also strive to keep their clients up-to-date on relevant industry trends so that lenders can remain competitive in a changing market. This could involve providing regular updates on interest rate changes or other new products that may be available. Money brokers should also use their expertise and industry connections to help clients navigate any potential issues or obstacles they may face throughout the loan process, as well as advice on debt management and budgeting strategies.

In addition, money brokers should provide unbiased advice when helping clients choose between different loan offers and recommending lenders to work with. Money brokers should investigate offers thoroughly to uncover hidden fees or high-interest rates which could cause long-term problems for the client in the future. By using ethical practices when dealing with lenders and clients, money brokers can build trust between themselves and reinforce their position as an expert source of advice within the industry.

Ultimately, money brokers must continue to provide ongoing support and guidance throughout all stages of the loan process to become successful in this field. By taking a client-focused approach while remaining mindful of potential risks, money brokers can effectively guide their clients towards achieving favorable terms while minimizing risk along the way.

Expanding your network of lenders and clients

Money brokers must develop an extensive network of lenders and clients to succeed in this lucrative industry. Money brokers should strive to create strong relationships with lenders as well as borrowers so that they can effectively negotiate the terms of loan agreements. Money brokers should also have a clear understanding of their clients' financial goals, needs, and capabilities to provide tailored advice and guidance.

Money brokers should take the initiative to build relationships with lenders by attending industry events or networking sessions. This will allow money brokers to introduce themselves to potential lenders who may be more willing to offer competitive rates for their clients' loans. Additionally, money brokers should connect with industry contacts through social media platforms such as LinkedIn or Twitter to create a larger network of contacts which could lead to more business opportunities.

In addition, money brokers should cultivate new relationships with borrowers by actively seeking out potential customers through marketing strategies such as email campaigns and online ads. Money brokers should emphasize the value they bring as well as their expertise within the industry when advertising their services. Furthermore, they should take the time to understand each borrower's individual financial situation and goals before making any recommendations on loan offers or lenders.

Ultimately, money brokers must continually expand their network of lenders and clients to become successful in this field. By taking an active approach towards building long-term relationships while emphasizing the value they bring to both parties, money brokers can maximize their earning potential while providing invaluable services for their clients.

Scaling your business and maximizing profitability

Money brokers must effectively scale their businesses to maximize profitability. Money brokers should have a clear understanding of their target market and the services they offer. They should know which products and services are most popular among their clients as well as what potential customers are looking for when seeking out a money broker. Having this knowledge will enable money brokers to focus their efforts on delivering the right services to the right people at the right time.

Money brokers should also strive to continually improve their customer service experience by providing quick responses to inquiries, timely follow-ups, and detailed explanations about the loan process. Money brokers should also be proactive in anticipating customer needs and addressing any potential issues that may arise throughout the loan application process. By providing quality customer service, money brokers can increase customer satisfaction levels while building trust with existing customers.

In addition, money brokers must be mindful of how they price their services to remain competitive within the industry. While it is important for money brokers to stay profitable, they must also ensure that their prices are affordable for clients without sacrificing quality of service. Money brokers can achieve this by offering different packages or payment plans that allow clients to select an option that suits their budget best while still receiving the same level of expertise from the money broker.

Finally, money brokers should always be prepared for unexpected costs or developments related to loan applications so that they can respond quickly when needed to minimize delays or disruptions to the process. This could involve having processes in place for handling late payments or changes in credit scores which could affect interest rates or terms of the loan agreement. Additionally, money brokers should keep up-to-date on relevant industry regulations which may change over time to ensure compliance with all laws governing lending practices within their region.

Ultimately, scaling a successful business as a money broker requires careful planning and preparation as well as an ongoing commitment towards improving and expanding services offered while staying ahead of industry trends and regulations. By following these strategies and leveraging available resources such as online tools or software programs designed specifically for this purpose, money brokers can become increasingly profitable while helping more clients successfully obtain loans with favorable terms and conditions.

Chapter 8: Overcoming Challenges and Building Long-Term Success

Being a successful money broker requires more than just understanding the industry and offering quality services. Money brokers must also be prepared to face different challenges that may arise along the way, as well as take steps to ensure their long-term success. In this chapter, we will discuss how money brokers can identify potential challenges, develop strategies for overcoming them, and build long-term success in their businesses. We will look at ways of managing difficult clients or lenders, dealing with unexpected costs or developments related to loan applications, staying ahead of industry trends and regulations, and leveraging available resources such as online tools or software programs designed specifically for this purpose. By following these strategies and taking proactive measures towards ensuring success in their business endeavors, money brokers can become increasingly profitable while helping more clients obtain loans with favorable terms and conditions.

Addressing common challenges faced by money brokers

Money brokers must effectively scale their businesses to maximize profitability. Money brokers should have a clear understanding of their target market and the services they offer. They should know which products and services are most popular among their clients as well as what potential customers are looking for when seeking out a money broker. Having this knowledge will enable money brokers to focus their efforts on delivering the right services to the right people at the right time while capitalizing on any potential opportunities that may arise in the industry.

In addition, money brokers should build relationships with lenders by researching various financial institutions and understanding different lending policies. This can help them identify potential lenders who may be more willing to offer competitive rates for their clients' loans. Additionally, money brokers should connect with industry contacts through social media platforms such as LinkedIn or Twitter to create a larger network of contacts which could lead to more business opportunities.

To successfully cultivate new relationships with borrowers, money brokers should use effective marketing strategies such as email campaigns and online ads. Money brokers should emphasize the value they bring as well as their expertise within the industry when advertising their services. Furthermore, they should take the time to understand each borrower's individual financial situation and goals before making any recommendations on loan offers or lenders, so that they can provide tailored recommendations that best suit each borrower's needs and budget.

Ultimately, money brokers must continually expand their network of lenders and clients to become successful in this field. By taking an active approach towards building long-term relationships while emphasizing the value they bring to both parties, money brokers can maximize their earning potential while providing invaluable services for their clients. It is also beneficial for money brokers to stay up-to-date on relevant industry regulations which may change over time as well as leverage available resources such as online tools or software programs designed specifically for this purpose to remain competitive within the market while staying compliant with all laws governing lending practices within their region.

Scaling your business and maximizing profitability also requires careful planning and preparation ahead of time in order ensure success down the line. Money brokers should develop systems and processes for handling customer inquiries quickly, responding to follow-up requests promptly, managing difficult clients or lenders if needed, dealing with unexpected costs or developments related to loan applications appropriately, staying ahead of industry trends and regulations, pricing services competitively but still profitably, anticipating customer needs accurately, addressing any potential issues that may arise throughout the loan application process swiftly, and leveraging available resources such as online tools or software programs designed specifically for this purpose efficiently. By following these strategies and taking proactive measures towards ensuring success in their business endeavors, money brokers can become increasingly profitable while helping more clients obtain loans with favorable terms and conditions over time leading them towards building long-term success in this field of work.

Strategies for overcoming competition and staying ahead in the industry

Money brokers should be aware of the competition in their industry and strive to stay ahead of the competition by leveraging their expertise. Money brokers should have extensive knowledge in this field, including understanding loan processes, loan policies, and regulations. They should also ensure that they are up-to-date on all relevant changes in the industry and any emerging trends. Additionally, money brokers should use various marketing techniques such as online ads or email campaigns to promote their services and reach more potential clients.

Money brokers should also focus on developing relationships with lenders as this will give them access to more competitive rates for loans. It is important for money brokers to research different lenders before selecting one to work with. This includes assessing lender's reputation, customer service policies, pricing structure, and credit requirements so that they can identify the best option for each borrower's financial situation. Money brokers must also take into account the fees associated with obtaining loans as these will directly affect their profitability.

At times, money brokers may face challenging situations while managing clients or lenders which could impact their reputation or business if not managed properly. Therefore, it is essential for money brokers to have effective strategies in place for handling difficult clients or lenders and resolving any issues that arise during the loan application process quickly and efficiently. Money brokers should also anticipate customer needs ahead of time so they can offer tailored solutions to each individual's unique financial situation while maintaining a high level of satisfaction.

Finally, money brokers should leverage available resources such as online tools or software programs designed specifically for this purpose to remain competitive within the market while staying compliant with all laws governing lending practices within their region at all times. By following these strategies and taking proactive measures towards ensuring success in their business endeavors, money brokers can maximize their earning potential while providing invaluable services for borrowers seeking low-interest rate loans over time leading them towards building long-term success in this field of work.

Adapting to changing market conditions and regulations

Money brokers must be able to adapt to changing market conditions and regulations to remain competitive in their industry. Money brokers should stay informed of the latest changes in the industry as well as any emerging trends to stay ahead of their competition and provide the best services for their clients. They should also have an understanding of the various policies, procedures, and laws governing lending practices within their region as this will allow them to comply with all relevant regulations while providing tailored recommendations that best suit each borrower's individual needs and budget.

It is also important for money brokers to continually update their skillset to remain a competitive player in the market. This includes acquiring knowledge on financial products such as mortgages, car loans, and more. Furthermore, money brokers should develop expertise in negotiation techniques so they can effectively negotiate with lenders for lower interest rates on behalf of their clientele. Additionally, money brokers must gain familiarity with online tools or software programs designed specifically for this purpose such as loan comparison platforms or credit score calculators which could help them streamline the loan process while making it easier for borrowers to make sound decisions based on accurate information about available loan options.

Moreover, money brokers should establish relationships with a wide range of lenders which could offer more varied options when searching for suitable loans. Such relationships may provide access to better interest rates or reduced fees which could then be passed onto clients' resulting in potential savings through lower loan payments over time. Money brokers should also take an active approach towards building long-term relationships with lenders by leveraging partnerships carefully while emphasizing the value they bring both parties.

Finally, money brokers should use data analytics tools such as risk assessment models or predictive analysis platforms when assessing borrowers' creditworthiness or eligibility for certain loan offers so that they can reduce any potential risks associated with loans taken out by clients while ensuring those chosen are most suitable given each borrower's specific financial situation. By utilizing these strategies and taking proactive measures towards staying competitive within the market, money brokers can maximize their earning potential while helping more clients obtain loans with favorable terms and conditions over time leading them towards building long-term success within this field.

Building a reputation for trust and reliability

Money brokers should strive to build a reputation for trust and reliability to be successful in the industry. Potential borrowers need to have confidence that money brokers can assist them in finding the most suitable loan options with competitive rates and terms. As such, money brokers must continually work on developing their expertise and demonstrate their dedication to helping clients find the best deal possible.

Money brokers should focus on understanding each client's financial situation in depth and use this information to tailor solutions that best suit their needs. This includes gathering details such as income, debt obligations, credit score, credit history, employment status, assets, liabilities, and other related factors so that they can accurately assess an individual's eligibility for different loan options while taking into account any special conditions or requirements associated with each. Furthermore, money brokers must be able to accurately evaluate lenders' offers based on factors like interest rates, repayment terms, fees, closing costs, duration of loan application process etc., so that they can identify the best option available for each borrower.

In addition to offering tailored recommendations, money brokers should stay up-to-date on all relevant changes in the field and have a strong understanding of any emerging trends to provide clients with accurate advice. Money brokers must also possess excellent communication skills as this will allow them to effectively negotiate with lenders on behalf of their clients while ensuring that all parties are satisfied with the outcome of a deal. Moreover, money brokers should ensure timely responses when communicating with both clients and lenders as this will help them build trust over time leading towards long-term relationships which could result in repeat business or referrals from satisfied customers.

Money brokers must also take steps towards complying with all laws governing lending practices within their region so as not to put themselves at risk of legal action or fines by authorities resulting from inappropriate or fraudulent practices during transactions between lenders and borrowers. Money brokers should also employ industry best practices such as using secure payment processing systems when handling payments made by clients or lenders which could help protect against potential frauds or identity thefts while providing peace of mind for all parties involved during loan dealings.

Finally, money brokers should always maintain ethical behavior throughout any business dealings they engage in as this will help protect their reputation and further strengthen relationships between themselves and their clientele. Money Brokers should strive towards keeping up these high standards on a consistent basis as it is essential for achieving success within this field over time while earning higher profits along the way.

Overall, becoming a successful money broker requires dedication and hard work. Money brokers must continually update their skillset to remain competitive within the market while also developing expertise in negotiating techniques which can be used to secure low-interest rates for clients. Additionally, money brokers should establish relationships with lenders so they have access to better loan options as well as leverage industry tools such as data analytics platforms when assessing borrowers' creditworthiness or eligibility for certain loans. Finally, money brokers must continuously build trust and reliability by adhering to ethical practices at all times whilst ensuring timely responses during dealings between themselves and both clientele and lenders alike. By following these strategies on an ongoing basis, aspiring money brokers will be able to maximize their earning potential while helping more people obtain suitable loans leading them towards long-term success in this field.

Chapter 9: Setting Up the Loan Application

This chapter provides aspiring money brokers with the necessary information and tips to help them set up a loan application for their clients. It covers topics such as understanding the loan application process, preparing documents needed for submission, determining eligibility requirements, gathering relevant financial information from borrowers, submitting applications to lenders and negotiating for lower interest rates. The book also emphasizes on the importance of taking an active approach towards staying competitive in the market while ensuring that all parties involved benefit from each transaction. By following these strategies and leveraging industry best practices when dealing with both lenders and clients alike, money brokers can maximize their earning potential while helping more people obtain suitable loans leading them towards long-term success in this field.

Explain the importance of setting up a loan application

Setting up a loan application is an important step in the money brokering process, as it helps establish each client's financial situation and eligibility for certain loan offers. Preparing an accurate and complete application will ensure that lenders consider the borrower's profile in depth when evaluating their request. The money broker should be well-versed with all aspects of the loan application process so that they can provide timely guidance to their clients.

The money broker should first assess their client's financial profile and background information as this will enable them to determine which loans are most suitable for them. This includes gathering details such as income, debt obligations, credit score, credit history, employment status, assets, liabilities, and other related factors so that they can accurately assess an individual's eligibility for different loan options while taking into account any special conditions or requirements associated with each.

Once this due diligence is completed, the money broker should help their client compile all documentation needed for submission such as bank statements, tax returns, pay stubs etc. The broker must also review these documents carefully to ensure accuracy and completeness before submitting them to lenders on behalf of their clients. Additionally, the money broker should assist their clientele in preparing personalized letters of explanation outlining any extenuating circumstances or discrepancies between their application data and statements that may be relevant when evaluating potential loan offers from lenders.

Money brokers must also be aware of key criteria used by lenders when assessing applications such as creditworthiness — based on factors like credit score, repayment history etc., debt-to-income ratio — calculated by dividing total monthly debt payments by gross monthly income etc., liquid assets — amount of cash available after settling all debts etc., employment status — proof of sustained full-time employment etc., required down payment — percentage of purchase price payable at closing - etc. Money brokers should use this information to create a comprehensive profile for each borrower which they can present to prospective lenders to maximize chances of approval while also obtaining better terms such as lower interest rates and more favorable repayment options on behalf of the borrower.

Finally, money brokers should utilize industry best practices when filing applications with lenders such as leveraging online tools which allow them to quickly submit multiple requests at once thus enabling faster turnaround times from borrowers; using data analytics platforms to accurately assess borrowers' creditworthiness; utilizing secure payment processing systems when handling payments made by clients or lenders; developing relationships with multiple lending partners so that they have access to better loan options; staying up-to-date on changes in regulations governing lending practices within the market; negotiating with lenders on behalf of clients whenever possible to secure lower interest rates; maintaining ethical behavior throughout dealings between themselves and both clients and lenders alike; ensuring timely responses during communication between parties involved during transactions; and taking steps towards complying with laws governing lending practices within the region at all times so as not to put themselves at risk of legal action or fines by authorities resulting from inappropriate or fraudulent practices during transactions between borrowers and lenders. All these measures taken together will help aspiring money brokers establish a successful career while earning higher profits along the way.

Outline the necessary steps for completing an effective loan application

The loan application process involves a number of steps that must be navigated to ensure an effective application and the highest chance of success. Money brokers must take an active role in guiding their clients through the entire procedure, from gathering all necessary documentation, assessing their creditworthiness, to negotiating with lenders for better terms.

The first step is to assess the client's financial profile and background information. This includes gathering details such as income, debt obligations, credit score, credit history, employment status, assets, liabilities and any other related factors which can help determine what loans are most suitable for them. It's also important to note any special conditions or requirements associated with each loan option that could influence the borrower's decision-making process.

Once this assessment is completed, money brokers should help their clients compile all documents needed for submission such as bank statements, tax returns, pay stubs etc. The broker must also review these documents carefully to ensure accuracy and completeness before submitting them to lenders on behalf of their clients. Additionally, the money broker should assist their clientele in preparing personalized letters of explanation outlining any extenuating circumstances or discrepancies between their application data and statements that may be relevant when evaluating potential loan offers from lenders.

After the initial paperwork has been submitted, brokers must then follow up with lenders to ensure they have received all required documentation and have made a decision regarding the borrower's eligibility for specific loan products offered by various financial institutions. They should remain vigilant throughout this process as it's critical that all information is kept updated so that timely decisions can be reached quickly and efficiently on behalf of borrowers seeking immediate financing solutions.

Money brokers should also leverage online tools which allow them to quickly submit multiple requests at once thus enabling faster turnaround times from borrowers; use data analytics platforms to accurately assess borrowers' creditworthiness; utilize secure payment processing systems when handling payments made by clients or lenders; develop relationships with multiple lending partners so that they have access to better loan options; stay up-to-date on changes in regulations governing lending practices within the market; negotiate with lenders on behalf of clients whenever possible to secure lower interest rates; maintain ethical behavior throughout dealings between themselves and both clients and lenders alike; ensure timely responses during communication between parties involved during transactions; and take steps towards complying with laws governing lending practices within the region at all times so as not to put themselves at risk of legal action or fines by authorities resulting from inappropriate or fraudulent practices during transactions between borrowers and lenders.

Finally, money brokers need to remember key criteria used by lenders when assessing applications such as creditworthiness — based on factors like credit score, repayment history etc., debt-to-income ratio — calculated by dividing total monthly debt payments by gross monthly income etc., liquid assets — the amount of cash available after settling all debts etc., employment status — proof of sustained full-time employment etc., required down payment — the percentage of purchase price payable at closing - etc.. Utilizing these criteria helps create a comprehensive profile for each borrower which they can present to prospective lenders to maximize chances of approval while also obtaining better terms such as lower interest rates and more favorable repayment options on behalf of the borrower. Understanding all aspects involved in setting up an effective loan application is essential for aspiring money brokers who wish to maximize their earning potential while helping more people obtain suitable loans leading them toward long-term success in this field.

Discuss how to gather all required information and documents from clients

Money brokers should take an active role in helping clients gather all required information and documentation needed for a successful loan application. This includes assessing their financial profile to determine what types of loans are most suitable, gathering bank statements, tax returns, pay stubs, and other important documents, as well as preparing letters of explanation outlining any extenuating circumstances or discrepancies between the borrower's application and statements.

For starters, money brokers should review the borrower's income, debt obligations, credit score and history, employment status, assets and liabilities. It is of paramount importance to ensure accuracy when evaluating the borrower's financial profile as this will determine the kinds of loans they qualify for. Money brokers must also be aware of special conditions associated with each loan option that could influence the borrower's decision-making process.

After assessing the financial profile, money brokers should help their clients compile all documents needed for loan submission such as bank statements (for at least two years), tax returns (for a minimum period of two years), pay stubs (for at least three months prior to making an application) etc. All these documents must be reviewed thoroughly before submitting them to potential lenders on behalf of their clientele. The money broker should also provide tailored letters or explanations stating any extenuating circumstances or discrepancies between what is indicated on their applications compared to those stated in their statements which could be relevant when considering potential loan offers from lenders.

In addition to this paperwork, it's important for money brokers to leverage online tools which allow them to quickly submit multiple requests at once thus enabling faster turnaround times from borrowers; use data analytics platforms accurately assess borrowers' creditworthiness; utilize secure payment processing systems when handling payments made by clients or lenders; develop relationships with multiple lending partners so that they have access to better loan options; stay up-to-date on changes in regulations governing lending practices within the market; negotiate with lenders on behalf of clients whenever possible to secure lower interest rates; maintain ethical behavior throughout dealings between themselves and both clients and lenders alike; ensure timely responses during communication between parties involved during transactions; and take steps towards complying with laws governing lending practices within the region at all times so as not to put themselves at risk of legal action or fines by authorities resulting from inappropriate or fraudulent practices during transactions between borrowers and lenders.

When gathering necessary information from clients, it is also important for aspiring money brokers to understand key criteria used by lenders when assessing applications such as creditworthiness — based on factors like credit score, repayment history etc., debt-to-income ratio — calculated by dividing total monthly debt payments by gross monthly income etc., liquid assets — amount of cash available after settling all debts etc., employment status — proof of sustained full-time employment etc., required down payment — percentage of purchase price payable at closing - etc.. Utilizing these criteria helps create a comprehensive profile for each borrower which can then be presented to prospective lenders to maximize chances of approval while obtaining better terms such as lower interest rates and more favorable repayment options on behalf of the borrower. Understanding all aspects involved in setting up an effective loan application is essential for aspiring money brokers who wish to maximize their earning potential while helping more people obtain suitable loans leading them toward long-term success in this field.

Money brokers must be prepared to submit comprehensive loan applications on behalf of their clients and have a thorough understanding of the process. This includes evaluating the borrower's financial profile to determine what types of loans are most suitable, gathering all necessary documents and information, and preparing letters of explanation for any extenuating circumstances.

Money brokers need to evaluate important factors like credit score and repayment history to determine the borrower's creditworthiness when analyzing their financial profile. Performing comprehensive research is crucial for money brokers to find loan options that offer favorable terms and fit the requirements of their clients. They should also be aware of special conditions associated with each loan option that could influence the borrower's decision-making process. For instance, some lenders may require higher down payments for certain types of loans or impose stricter requirements for borrowers who are self-employed or have recently changed jobs. Money brokers should make sure they are familiar with all aspects related to different loan options so they can present potential solutions tailored to their client's specific needs.

Money brokers should also help their clients compile all documents needed for submitting a successful application such as bank statements (for at least two years), tax returns (for a minimum period of two years), pay stubs (for at least three months before making an application) etc. All these documents must be reviewed thoroughly before submitting them to prospective lenders on behalf of their clientele. It is also important for money brokers to provide tailored letters or explanations highlighting any extenuating circumstances or discrepancies between what is indicated on their applications compared to those stated in their statements which could be relevant when considering potential loan offers from lenders.

In addition to this paperwork, it's important for money brokers to leverage online tools which allow them to quickly submit multiple requests at once thus enabling faster turnaround times from borrowers; use data analytics platforms accurately assess borrowers' creditworthiness; utilize secure payment processing systems when handling payments made by clients or lenders; develop relationships with multiple lending partners so that they have access to better loan options; stay up-to-date on changes in regulations governing lending practices within the market; negotiate with lenders on behalf of clients whenever possible to secure lower interest rates; maintain ethical behavior throughout dealings between themselves and both clients and lenders alike; ensure timely responses during communication between parties involved during transactions; and take steps towards complying with laws governing lending practices within the region at all times so as not to put themselves at risk of legal action or fines by authorities resulting from inappropriate or fraudulent practices during transactions between borrowers and lenders.

After gathering all necessary information and documents from clients, aspiring money brokers should ensure accuracy when completing each respective section on the application form while being mindful not only of potential risks associated with incorrect answers but also opportunities that can arise through proper disclosure throughout the process leading towards successful outcomes for both themselves and their clientele. Moreover, it is important for money brokers to keep track of changes in regulations associated with different types loans as well as assessing whether new products available in the market better suit their clients' needs since this could potentially lead towards more favorable terms than originally considered such as lower interest rates or more flexible repayment plans etc., ultimately helping aspiring money brokers build long-term success while providing invaluable assistance leading people towards achieving financial stability.

Best practices for responding to lenders' requests during the approval process

Money brokers must also be prepared to respond to lenders' requests during the approval process. It is important for money brokers to stay organized, track all documents and communications, and ensure timely responses to facilitate a smooth process that can lead to successful outcomes. Best practices for money brokers when dealing with lenders include doing their due diligence by understanding each lender's requirements before submitting applications on behalf of clients. This includes taking into account factors like loan type (e.g., mortgage, home equity line of credit, etc.), liquid assets, employment status, required down payment percentage etc.

In addition to this, it is essential for money brokers to review the documents submitted by borrowers carefully before submitting them to lenders so as not to provide incorrect or incomplete information which could prevent an application from being approved. Money brokers need to be aware of any discrepancies between what was reported on the application and what was stated in the borrower's statements which could potentially affect a lender's decision regarding approval or denial of the loan request. For example, if the income or asset information provided on the application does not match what was stated in the borrower's bank statements then additional explanation might be requested by a lender prior to making a final decision.

It is also important for money brokers to remain professional and courteous when communicating with lenders throughout every stage of the loan application process as this will help create positive relationships that could benefit both parties in future transactions. If mistakes are made or certain conditions cannot be met then it is important for money brokers to apologize and take responsibility to maintain trust with lenders.

Finally, aspiring money brokers should make sure they comply with applicable laws regulating loan origination within their region at all times regardless of whether this involves transactions between themselves and individual borrowers or business entities such as banks and other financial institutions. They should also make sure they are familiar with fair lending requirements according to federal regulations that prohibit discrimination based on race/ethnicity, age, gender etc., to comply with local regulations while protecting clients' rights from potential exploitation at all times. Taking all these steps correctly will help aspiring money brokers succeed professionally while helping others achieve their financial goals towards long-term success as a profitable money brokers.

Highlight ways money brokers can ensure accuracy when submitting applications

Money brokers often find themselves in a unique position in which they are acting as the middleman between lenders and borrowers. As such, aspiring money brokers need to have an understanding of the loan application process to ensure accuracy when completing applications on behalf of clients.

The first step is to gather all relevant documents and information from clients such as credit reports, tax returns, employment and income records, bank statements, and other supporting documents. Money brokers need to review these thoroughly to verify if the information provided is accurate and up-to-date before applying. Additionally, aspiring money brokers should also be aware of any risks associated with providing incorrect or incomplete information that could lead to potential problems down the line.

When completing an application, money brokers need to pay close attention to details and make sure all data entered is correct. This includes double-checking information such as names, contact details, addresses and even dates of birth to avoid any potential errors when submitting applications on behalf of clients. Another important aspect to remember is that lenders usually require exact figures and not rounded-up numbers so aspiring money brokers must ensure accuracy when providing this type of detail as well.

Finally, before applying, it's also essential for money brokers to go over all documents once again with their clients to confirm the accuracy and provide explanations regarding any questions or concerns they may have about the process. By taking all of these steps and ensuring accuracy when submitting loan applications, money brokers can help their clients succeed in obtaining the financing they need while building a successful career as a profitable money broker.

Provide tips for staying organized throughout the entire loan application process

Money brokers must be highly organized and attentive throughout the entire loan application process to facilitate successful outcomes for their clients. Aspiring money brokers need to stay on top of documents and communications by keeping detailed records of each step in the process to ensure accuracy and remain compliant with regulations.

To stay organized, money brokers should create a workflow system that outlines every step from start to finish. They should also take advantage of technology such as cloud-based software solutions that can help them track all relevant information such as emails, documents, notes, tasks, client details etc. This type of system will help money brokers manage the process more efficiently while reducing potential mistakes or issues that could arise due to lack of organization.

It's also important for money brokers to keep their clients informed throughout the process so they know the status of their applications at any given point. Regular communication is key here so money brokers need to use a reliable method (e.g., email or phone) that ensures timely responses and updates. Money brokers must also keep accurate records regarding when lenders have requested additional documents or clarification to avoid delays that could result from not providing this information promptly.

In addition to this, aspiring money brokers should be sure to stay up-to-date with industry news and changes in regulations so they are aware of any new requirements or procedures that need to be followed during the loan application process. They should attend conferences and seminars or read up on publications related to their field to stay abreast of developments that could affect how they handle applications on behalf of their clients.

Finally, taking time out for self-care is essential for aspiring money brokers since staying organized often requires long hours behind a desk or engaging in stressful conversations with lenders or clients alike. They need to remember to take regular breaks throughout the day and set aside time for activities outside of work such as exercise, socializing, hobbies etc., which can help them maintain focus when dealing with complex situations associated with loan origination processes. By following these tips, aspiring money brokers can ensure accuracy while remaining organized throughout the entire loan application process on behalf of their clients while setting themselves up for success as profitable money brokers over time.

Becoming a profitable money broker requires dedication and hard work, but it can be incredibly rewarding. Understanding the industry, developing necessary skills, setting up a business, building networks of lenders and clients, navigating the loan application process accurately while staying organized throughout the entire process as well as taking time for self-care are all steps aspiring money brokers must take to achieve long-term success. With these tips in mind, anyone with an entrepreneurial spirit should be able to make their mark on this exciting field and become a successful money broker over time.

Chapter 10: How Do Money Brokers Get Paid?

Money brokers are professionals who provide financial services to clients by helping them secure the best loan terms and rates. They often do this by connecting borrowers with lenders, negotiating on their behalf, and managing the entire process until a successful outcome is reached. But how exactly do money brokers get paid for their services? In this chapter, we will explore different methods of payment available to money brokers as well as some tips for maximizing profits to make a living off of providing these valuable services.

Overview of Money Brokers and How They Get Paid

With the rise of new technologies and companies providing financial services, money brokers have more opportunities to make money than ever before. They can sign up as independent contractors with companies such as Upstart or LendingClub, help clients find private lenders such as peer-to-peer lending networks, or even set up their own brokerage business to become an entrepreneur in the financial services sector. Regardless of which route they take, money brokers will need to understand the different methods available for getting paid to maximize their earnings.

The most common method of payment for money brokers is through commission-based fees. This type of reimbursement typically consists of a percentage based on the total loan amount that clients agree to pay for utilizing the broker's services. It is important to note that due to state laws and regulations, some states prohibit money brokers from charging more than 1% commission on loans.

Another way that money brokers can get paid is by working on a retainer basis. Under this system, clients agree to pay a fixed fee upfront for money brokers to provide advice and assistance during the loan process. This type of payment structure is often best suited for individuals who are working with high-net-worth clients or those who are seeking long-term assistance with complex financial services issues. Retainer fees can range anywhere from $1,000 - $5,000 depending on the nature of the project and any additional tasks that may be required along the way.

In addition to these two payment structures, there are also other methods available for earning income as a money broker such as hourly rates or flat fees. Money brokers should carefully consider which payment method works best for them depending on how much time they plan to invest into helping their clients secure financing and what types of services they offer (e.g., managing paperwork versus arranging meetings). In some cases, it may even be possible to negotiate alternative payment arrangements if both parties are open-minded and flexible when it comes to finding an agreement that works for everyone involved.

Overall, becoming a successful money broker requires dedication and hard work but it can be incredibly rewarding when done right. Money brokers must stay up-to-date with industry news and changes in regulations as well as understand different methods available for getting paid to maximize their potential earnings over time. With these tips in mind, anyone with an entrepreneurial spirit should be able to leverage their skillset and knowledge into making a living off providing valuable financial services while building long-term success as a profitable money broker over time.

How Money Brokers Negotiate Their Pay From Clients

Money brokers must negotiate their fees with clients to make a living off of providing financial services. Negotiating these fees is an important step for money brokers since it will help them determine how much income they can expect to earn from their services.

When negotiating fees, money brokers should be sure to clearly define what services they will provide and any expectations that both parties have in terms of the outcome. It's also important for them to understand the market rate for money broker services, as this will help them determine a fair fee that is suitable for both parties. Additionally, it's wise to create a written agreement that outlines the details of their services to protect both parties involved should a dispute arise.

Money brokers may also want to consider offering discounts or special pricing models to attract more clients and increase their earnings potential. For instance, some money brokers may offer sliding scale rates based on the client's income bracket or offer discounts when multiple loans are requested at once. Other money brokers may choose to charge an hourly rate instead of a commission-based fee to give clients more flexibility when it comes to paying their fees.

Ultimately, successful negotiations between money brokers and their clients involve understanding each other's needs and working together toward an agreement that is beneficial for both parties. Money brokers should remember that while negotiation can be challenging at times, it is also essential in helping them reach agreements with new and existing clients which will enable them to make a living off of providing valuable financial services over time.

Understanding Loan Origination Fees

Money brokers may also find themselves dealing with a loan origination fee. This is an additional fee charged by the lender on top of the interest rate on the loan. The loan origination fee is used to cover certain administrative costs associated with processing the loan, such as the cost of verifying documents, preparing and filing paperwork, and other related services. This fee can range from 0.5% to 2% of the total loan amount and is generally paid up front when the loan is approved.

In some cases, money brokers may be able to negotiate a lower origination fee for their clients as part of their negotiation process. In addition to reducing overall fees associated with the loan, this can help money brokers build better relationships with their clients and create stronger loyalty over time. To reduce origination fees successfully, money brokers must have strong knowledge of industry standards and be able to leverage their negotiation skills to get a favorable outcome for both parties involved in the transaction.

Money brokers may also be able to increase their potential earnings by offering additional services beyond just helping clients obtain loans. For example, they could provide advice on budgeting, credit score improvement, debt management plans, or other related financial matters that could help their clients save more money in the long run. By providing these extra services as part of their service package, money brokers can charge higher fees for taking on more responsibility which can result in greater profits over time.

Finally, being successful as a money broker requires staying abreast of industry trends and changes in regulations that could affect how they do business or how they earn income from providing financial services. Money brokers should take advantage of continuing education opportunities such as online courses or attending conferences to stay up-to-date with any changes that occur to remain competitive within the industry and maintain a profitable business model over time.

Benefits of Becoming a Money Broker

Answer: Becoming a money broker can be an incredibly rewarding and lucrative career path. Money brokers are responsible for helping their clients find low-interest rate loans from various lenders, acting as a middleman between the two parties, and handling all of the paperwork involved in the loan process. By becoming a money broker, individuals can make up to $100,000/year by leveraging their financial expertise and knowledge to provide valuable service to their clients.

When entering the money broker industry, it's important to understand the different facets of the business including how to negotiate fees with clients, understand loan origination fees, manage client expectations, and build relationships with lenders. It's also essential for aspiring money brokers to develop necessary skills such as communication, problem-solving, financial literacy, and negotiation to maximize their potential earnings over time. Additionally, knowing how to establish a business and create a network of lenders and clients is paramount for success as a money broker.

Money brokers must also be able to navigate the loan application process including filing out paperwork correctly and on time while ensuring that all documents meet regulatory requirements. Additionally, they must be knowledgeable about different types of loans available so that they can advise their clients on selecting an appropriate loan product based on their individual needs and circumstances. Negotiating for low-interest rates is also an important skill that will help money brokers earn more income as they will be able to secure better deals for their clients which could result in repeat business over time.

Finally, managing and growing their businesses is essential for long-term success as a money broker. This includes streamlining operations so that transactions are processed quickly and efficiently while keeping costs down; increasing efficiency by utilizing technology; developing marketing strategies; setting goals; creating systems; hiring personnel when needed; staying up-to-date with industry news; understanding different methods available for getting paid (e.g., hourly rates or flat fees); offering discounts or special pricing models; providing additional services beyond just finding loans (e.g., budgeting advice); taking advantage of continuing education opportunities such as online courses or attending conferences; maintaining strong relationships with lenders and clients over time by providing excellent customer service; overcoming challenges when possible; monitoring performance metrics such as number of successful transactions or average interest rate negotiated per client; learning how to deal with disappointment gracefully if any negotiations fail due unforeseen circumstances etc.; understanding different legal implications involved in handling financial issues related to loans etc.; continuing to build networks through networking events etc.; leveraging one's entrepreneurial spirit into making decisions that will benefit both oneself and one's customers etc.. All these skills combined make becoming a profitable money broker achievable overtime with dedication and hard work being key factors in achieving success within this industry.

Tips for Maximizing Earnings as a Money Broker

Becoming a money broker can be an incredibly rewarding and lucrative career path, with the potential to earn up to $100,000/year for those willing to dedicate time and effort into mastering the business. Money brokers serve as a middleman between lenders and borrowers by helping clients find low-interest rate loans from various lenders and managing all of the paperwork involved in the loan process. To maximize one's potential earnings, it's important to develop several key skills such as communication, problem-solving, financial literacy, negotiation, and understanding the different types of loans available.

Money brokers should also have strong knowledge of industry standards and regulations as well as an understanding of loan origination fees. They should be able to leverage their negotiation skills to get a favorable outcome for both parties involved in the transaction while reducing overall fees associated with the loan. In addition, money brokers can increase their income potential by offering additional services beyond just finding loans such as providing advice on budgeting, credit score improvement, or debt management plans. Money brokers must stay abreast of industry trends and changes in regulations that could affect how they do business or how they earn income from providing financial services - taking advantage of continuing education opportunities such as online courses or attending conferences can help them do this.

To make sure money broker businesses remain profitable over time, it's important for them to focus on streamlining operations so that transactions are processed quickly and efficiently; using technology to increase efficiency; developing marketing strategies; setting goals; creating systems; hiring personnel when needed; maintaining strong relationships with lenders and clients over time by providing excellent customer service; overcoming challenges when possible; monitoring performance metrics such as a number of successful transactions or average interest rate negotiated per client; learning how to deal with disappointment gracefully if any negotiations fail due unforeseen circumstances etc.; understanding different legal implications involved in handling financial issues related to loans etc.; continuing to build networks through networking events etc.; leveraging one's entrepreneurial spirit into making decisions that will benefit both oneself and one's customers etc.. Working hard while recognizing opportunities for growth will position aspiring money brokers on track towards achieving success in this field.

Challenges to Overcome When Starting Out as a Money Broker

Starting as a money broker can be a daunting task with several challenges that must be overcome to ensure success. Money brokers must understand the industry and develop necessary skills such as communication, negotiation, problem-solving, financial literacy, understanding different types of loans available, and having an awareness of the regulatory environment. They must also build a network of lenders and clients which can be done through referrals or using online resources. Money brokers should also create systems for managing their business efficiently to maximize profits including streamlining operations so that transactions are processed quickly; using technology to increase efficiency; developing marketing strategies; setting goals; creating systems; hiring personnel when needed etc.

Furthermore, money brokers should stay up-to-date with industry news and changes in regulations that could affect how they do business or how they earn income from providing financial services. Taking advantage of continuing education opportunities such as online courses or attending conferences can help them do this. Understanding different methods available for getting paid (e.g., hourly rates or flat fees); offering discounts or special pricing models; providing additional services beyond just finding loans (e.g., budgeting advice); and learning how to handle disappointment in a dignified manner if negotiations do not succeed due to unexpected events or other reasons; Understanding the different legal implications involved in handling financial issues related to loans, etc.; continuing to build networks through networking events, etc.; leveraging one's entrepreneurial spirit to make decisions that will benefit both oneself and one's customers, etc. With dedication and hard work being key factors in achieving success in this industry, all these skills combined make it achievable to become a profitable money broker over time.

In addition, money brokers should be aware of the potential risks associated with this type of profession such as loan fraud or failure to comply with state and federal laws which could lead to costly lawsuits and fines. Financial institutions may also refuse to lend funds if they believe the proposed terms are too risky or questionable which could result in lost business opportunities or failed negotiations for money brokers. Finally, competition can be fierce in the brokerage industry as there may be other professionals vying for the same clients who offer better deals than yours. To stand out above competitors, money brokers should focus on building relationships and trust with lenders and clients by providing excellent customer service so that you become their go-to resource when seeking low-interest rate loans.

Final Words

Becoming a successful money broker can be an incredibly rewarding career path with great potential for earning significant income. It involves understanding the industry and developing key skills such as communication, problem-solving, financial literacy, negotiation, and knowledge of loan origination fees. Money brokers should also stay up to date on industry trends and changes in regulations that could affect how they do business or earn income from providing financial services. Finally, it's important to focus on streamlining operations so transactions are processed quickly; leveraging one's entrepreneurial spirit into making decisions that will benefit both oneself and customers; building relationships through excellent customer service; overcoming challenges when possible; monitoring performance metrics, etc., all while recognizing growth opportunities which will position aspiring money brokers towards achieving success in this field. With dedication and hard work being the two primary ingredients required for becoming a profitable money broker, there is no limit to what you can achieve!

Valuable Resources for Aspiring Money Brokers

Here are some valuable website references you can go to learn more about operating as a money broker:

1. Investopedia -> https://www.investopedia.com
2. Bankrate -> https://www.bankrate.com
3. NerdWallet -> https://www.nerdwallet.com
4. FinanceTraining.com -> https://financetraining.com
5. Loans Broker Blog -> https://loansbrokerblog.com
6. BiggerPockets -> https://www.biggerpockets.com
7. Mortgage Professionals America -> https://www.mpamag.com
8. Mortgage News Daily -> http://www.mortgagenewsdaily.com
9. LoanOfficerSchool.com -> https://www.loanofficerschool.com
10. National Association of Mortgage Brokers -> https://www.namb.org
11. Udemy -> https://www.udemy.com
12. Coursera -> https://www.coursera.org
13. LinkedIn Learning -> https://www.linkedin.com/learning
14. National Mortgage News -> https://www.nationalmortgagenews.com
15. Mortgage Bankers Association -> https://www.mba.org
16. Loan Broker Forums -> https://loanbrokerforums.com
17. HousingWire -> https://www.housingwire.com

18. Loan Officer Hub -> https://loanofficerhub.com
19. Finance Broker Association of Australia -> https://www.fbaa.com.au
20. Khan Academy -> https://www.khanacademy.org
21. Alison -> https://alison.com
22. Loan Officer Freedom -> https://loanofficerfreedom.com
23. Edx -> https://www.edx.org
24. Real Estate Institute of Australia -> https://www.reia.com.au
25. Finance and Mortgage Broking Interactive -> http://financeandmortgagebroking.com.au
26. The Truth About Mortgage -> https://www.thetruthaboutmortgage.com
27. Reddit - /r/Mortgage -> https://www.reddit.com/r/Mortgage
28. Reddit - /r/Loans -> https://www.reddit.com/r/Loans
29. Commercial Loan Direct -> https://www.commercialloandirect.com
30. Mortgage Professional Australia -> https://www.mpamag.com/au
31. Loan Officer Training -> https://loanofficertraining.com
32. Australian Finance Group -> https://www.afgonline.com.au
33. Mortgage Coach -> https://mortgagecoach.com
34. Finance Brokers Association of Australia -> https://www.fbaa.com.au

35. Mortgage Training Institute -> https://www.mortgageknowledge.com
36. Institute of Financial Services -> https://www.libf.ac.uk
37. Mortgage101 -> https://www.mortgage101.com
38. LoanToolbox -> https://loantoolbox.com
39. Mortgage Educators -> https://mortgageeducators.com
40. The Institute of Financial Services -> https://www.libf.ac.uk
41. Origination News -> https://originationnews.com
42. Mortgage Strategy -> https://www.mortgagestrategy.co.uk
43. Broker Universe -> https://www.brokeruniverse.com
44. National Association of Mortgage Underwriters -> https://www.mortgage-underwriters.org
45. The Mortgage Collaborative -> https://www.mortgagecollaborative.com
46. School of Mortgage Banking -> https://www.mba.org/store/products/certifications-and-designations/school-of-mortgage-banking
47. Canadian Association of Accredited Mortgage Professionals -> https://www.mortgageproscan.ca
48. The Mortgage Training Center -> https://www.themortgagetrainingcenter.com
49. Loan Officer Magazine -> https://loanofficermagazine.com

50. American Banker -> https://www.americanbanker.com
51. Skillshare -> https://www.skillshare.com
52. The Knowledge Coop -> https://www.knowledgecoop.com
53. Fannie Mae - Training and Learning Resources -> https://singlefamily.fanniemae.com/learning-center
54. Zillow for Pros Blog -> [https://www.zillow.com/agent-resources
55. Total Mortgage Blog -> https://www.totalmortgage.com/blog
56. Mortgage Women Magazine -> https://www.mortgagewomenmagazine.com
57. Mortgage Fraud Blog -> https://www.mortgagefraudblog.com
58. Mortgage Compliance Magazine -> https://www.mortgagecompliancemagazine.com
59. Loan Market -> https://www.loanmarket.com.au
60. Loan Officer Success -> https://loanofficersuccess.com
61. Jungo - Mortgage CRM -> https://ijungo.com
62. Finance Ladder -> https://financeladder.net
63. Mortgage Introducer -> https://www.mortgageintroducer.com
64. Banking Exchange -> https://www.bankingexchange.com
65. ProBroker -> https://probroker.com
66. Global Banking & Finance Review -> https://www.globalbankingandfinance.com

67. The National Association of Commercial Finance Brokers -> https://www.nacfb.org
68. Finance Monthly -> https://www.finance-monthly.com
69. Future of Customer Engagement and Commerce -> https://www.the-future-of-commerce.com
70. Inside Mortgage Finance -> https://www.insidemortgagefinance.com
71. Finextra -> https://www.finextra.com
72. Financial Post -> https://financialpost.com
73. Bobsguide -> https://www.bobsguide.com
74. The Adviser - Australian Broker News -> https://www.theadviser.com.au
75. Scotsman Guide -> https://www.scotsmanguide.com
76. Mortgage Compliance Magazine -> https://www.mortgagecompliancemagazine.com
77. The Mortgage Reports -> https://themortgagereports.com
78. The Loan Consultants, Inc -> https://www.the-loan-consultants.com
79. Business Insider -> https://www.businessinsider.com
80. Forbes - Personal Finance Section -> https://www.forbes.com/personal-finance
81. The Balance -> https://www.thebalance.com
82. Mortgage Professional America -> https://www.mpamag.com
83. Canadian Mortgage Professionals -> https://www.canadianmortgagepro.com
84. National Mortgage Professional Magazine -> https://nationalmortgageprofessional.com

85. Real Estate Bees -> https://realestatebees.com
86. American Association of Private Lenders -> https://aaplonline.com
87. Mortgage Coach -> https://mortgagecoach.com
88. The Mortgage Leader -> https://themortgageleader.com
89. Loan Post -> https://loanpost.com
90. The American College of Financial Services -> https://www.theamericancollege.edu
91. EduMark -> https://edumark.com
92. Lending Times -> https://lending-times.com
93. Brokers That Profit -> https://brokersthatprofit.com
94. Loan Broker Guide -> https://loanbrokerguide.com
95. FinTech Futures -> https://www.fintechfutures.com
96. CFPB - Consumer Financial Protection Bureau -> https://www.consumerfinance.gov
97. Open Mortgage -> https://openmortgage.com

Super Special Bonus

Links to find side hustle to make even more money from home:

1. ProBlogger Job Board -> https://problogger.com/jobs/
2. Upwork -> https://www.upwork.com/
3. Fiverr -> https://www.fiverr.com/
4. Indeed -> https://www.indeed.com/
5. Freelancer -> https://www.freelancer.com/
6. LinkedIn -> https://www.linkedin.com/
7. TaskRabbit -> https://www.taskrabbit.com/
8. Etsy -> https://www.etsy.com/
9. Amazon Mechanical Turk -> https://www.mturk.com/
10. Glassdoor -> https://www.glassdoor.com/
11. eBay -> https://www.ebay.com/
12. Poshmark -> https://poshmark.com/
13. Rev -> https://www.rev.com/
14. Clickworker -> https://www.clickworker.com/
15. Toptal -> https://www.toptal.com/
16. Flexjobs -> https://www.flexjobs.com/
17. UserTesting -> https://www.usertesting.com/
18. Shopify -> https://www.shopify.com/
19. Guru -> https://www.guru.com/
20. Remote.co -> https://remote.co/
21. Monster -> https://www.monster.com/
22. Virtual Vocations -> https://www.virtualvocations.com/
23. We Work Remotely -> https://weworkremotely.com/
24. Rover -> https://www.rover.com/
25. Amazon Handmade -> https://www.amazon.com/handmade
26. Care.com -> https://www.care.com/

27. JustAnswer -> https://www.justanswer.com/
28. Zirtual -> https://www.zirtual.com/
29. Teachable -> https://www.teachable.com/
30. Udemy -> https://www.udemy.com/
31. Coursera -> https://www.coursera.org/
32. Skillshare -> https://www.skillshare.com/
33. Tutor.com -> https://www.tutor.com/
34. Chegg Tutors -> https://www.chegg.com/tutors/
35. VIPKid -> https://www.vipkid.com/
36. Outschool -> https://www.outschool.com/
37. Preply -> https://preply.com/
38. Italki -> https://www.italki.com/
39. Verblio -> https://www.verblio.com/
40. Textbroker -> https://www.textbroker.com/
41. Wise Bread -> https://www.wisebread.com/
42. The Penny Hoarder -> https://www.thepennyhoarder.com/
43. Money Saving Mom -> https://www.moneysavingmom.com/
44. The Work at Home Woman -> https://www.theworkathomewoman.com/
45. Real Ways to Earn -> https://realwaystoearnmoneyonline.com/
46. Work at Home Adventures -> https://wahadventures.com/
47. Work at Home Mom Revolution -> https://workathomemomrevolution.com/
48. Dream Home Based Work -> https://www.dreamhomebasedwork.com/
49. Remote OK -> https://remoteok.io/
50. Aquent -> https://aquent.com/

51. 99Designs -> https://99designs.com/
52. DesignCrowd -> https://www.designcrowd.com/
53. Crowdspring -> https://www.crowdspring.com/
54. CafePress -> https://www.cafepress.com/
55. Zazzle -> https://www.zazzle.com/
56. Society6 -> https://society6.com/
57. Threadless -> https://www.threadless.com/
58. Printful -> https://www.printful.com/
59. Redbubble -> https://www.redbubble.com/
60. TeeSpring -> https://teespring.com/
61. Lulu -> https://www.lulu.com/
62. CreateSpace -> https://www.createspace.com/
63. KDP -> https://kdp.amazon.com/
64. Blurb -> https://www.blurb.com/
65. Smashwords -> https://www.smashwords.com/
66. Leanpub -> https://leanpub.com/
67. BookBaby -> https://www.bookbaby.com/
68. Appen -> https://appen.com/
69. Lionbridge -> https://www.lionbridge.com/
70. TTEC -> https://www.ttecjobs.com/
71. Kelly Services -> https://www.kellyservices.us/
72. Working Solutions -> https://workingsolutions.com/
73. Liveops -> https://www.liveops.com/
74. The Social Element -> https://thesocialelement.agency/
75. Belay -> https://belaysolutions.com/

76. ArtFire -> https://www.artfire.com/
77. Spreadshirt -> https://www.spreadshirt.com/
78. Teefury -> https://www.teefury.com/
79. Merch by Amazon -> https://merch.amazon.com/landing
80. Adobe Stock -> https://stock.adobe.com/
81. Shutterstock -> https://www.shutterstock.com/
82. iStock -> https://www.istockphoto.com/
83. Getty Images -> https://www.gettyimages.com/
84. Alamy -> https://www.alamy.com/
85. 123RF -> https://www.123rf.com/
86. Dreamstime -> https://www.dreamstime.com/
87. Bigstock -> https://www.bigstockphoto.com/
88. CanStockPhoto -> https://www.canstockphoto.com/
89. Stocksy -> https://www.stocksy.com/
90. Pond5 -> https://www.pond5.com/
91. Twenty20 -> https://www.twenty20.com/
92. Depositphotos -> https://depositphotos.com/
93. Foap -> https://www.foap.com/
94. Scoopshot -> https://www.scoopshot.com/
95. Picfair -> https://www.picfair.com/
96. EyeEm -> https://www.eyeem.com/
97. Paid Forum Posting -> https://www.paidforumposting.com/
98. Postloop -> https://www.postloop.com/
99. TranscribeMe -> https://www.transcribeme.com/
100. Scribie -> https://scribie.com/

101. Quicktate -> https://quicktate.com/
102. Speechpad -> https://www.speechpad.com/
103. TranscriptionHub -> https://www.transcriptionhub.com/
104. Athreon -> https://www.athreon.com/
105. Gengo -> https://gengo.com/
106. Unbabel -> https://unbabel.com/
107. One Hour Translation -> https://www.onehourtranslation.com/
108. ProZ -> http://www.proz.com/
109. TranslatorsCafe -> https://www.translatorscafe.com/
110. Mars Solutions -> https://www.marssolutions.net/
111. Music Xray -> https://www.musicxray.com/
112. Slice the Pie -> https://www.slicethepie.com/
113. HitPredictor -> https://www.hitpredictor.com/
114. RadioLoyalty -> https://radioloyalty.com/
115. Research.fm -> https://research.fm/index.aspx
116. Userlytics -> https://www.userlytics.com/
117. TryMyUI -> https://www.trymyui.com/
118. UserFeel -> https://www.userfeel.com/
119. Validately -> https://www.validately.com/
120. TestingTime -> https://www.testingtime.com/
121. UserBrain -> https://www.userbrain.net/
122. Taskworld -> https://taskworld.com/
123. Hubstaff Talent -> https://talent.hubstaff.com/
124. AngelList -> https://angel.co/
125. Doordash -> https://www.doordash.com/
126. Grubhub -> https://www.grubhub.com/
127. Postmates -> https://postmates.com/

128. Instacart -> https://www.instacart.com/
129. Shipt -> https://www.shipt.com/
130. Decluttr -> https://www.decluttr.com/
131. Gazelle -> https://www.gazelle.com/
132. Swappa -> https://swappa.com/
133. Tradesy -> https://www.tradesy.com/
134. ThredUP -> https://www.thredup.com/
135. Flywheel -> https://getflywheel.com/
136. Bluehost -> https://www.bluehost.com/
137. SiteGround -> https://www.siteground.com/
138. Hostgator -> https://www.hostgator.com/
139. WPEngine -> https://wpengine.com/
140. Squarespace -> https://www.squarespace.com/
141. Wix -> https://www.wix.com/
142. JustHost -> https://www.justhost.com/
143. A2 Hosting -> https://www.a2hosting.com/
144. DreamHost -> https://www.dreamhost.com/
145. GreenGeeks -> https://www.greengeeks.com/
146. InMotion Hosting -> https://www.inmotionhosting.com/
147. Kinsta -> https://kinsta.com/
148. Cloudways -> https://www.cloudways.com/
149. WPX Hosting -> https://wpx.net/
150. Liquid Web -> https://www.liquidweb.com/

www.ingramcontent.com/pod-product-compliance
Lightning Source LLC
Chambersburg PA
CBHW062116220526
45471CB00010B/3757